MW00782097

PRAISE FOR JOURNEY IN THE PRESENT

"Tom Matson, author of *Unfrozen*, once again brilliantly takes us on a journey with humanity. He engages us in the complex dance of creating a values-based life. A process that is filled with hope, love, pain, reflection, growth and inspiration. Engage and enjoy the adventure."

-Tim Homan,
Father/Life Coach

"Tom Matson's authenticity is woven through personal narratives that invite the reader to share in his life experiences. These narratives, coupled with questions for reflection, create an opportunity for readers to unpack their own thoughts, feelings and questions about the life they are leading and who they want to become."

-Jaime Gaard Chapman,
Student-Athlete Development Coach

"*Journey in the Present* is a beautiful mosaic of Tom's personal leadership narratives and expertise in positive psychology. It's a simple, powerful guide for anyone seeking more truth in life."

-Rachel Williams,
Human Resources Executive

"In the current trend of American culture, Tom Matson has written a countercultural gem. *Journey in the Present* hits on a number of important themes like savoring, being in the moment, balance and learned optimism. These themes are approached through his willingness to be vulnerable and authentic. We are reminded that none of us are immune to adversity in this life, and instead of wishing for different circumstances, we ought to meet the adversity head-on and search for the greater meaning in it and the good that can come from it... even amidst painful struggle, Carpe Diem."

-Dr. Brandon Orr,
Sports Psychology Consultant & Professor

"*Journey in the Present* is a moving legacy that challenges each of us, without judgment, to stop wherever we are, identify our values and evaluate whether we are operating in alignment therewith."

-Andrea Hedtke,
Attorney and Lucky Mama to Three Beautiful Girls

"*Journey in the Present* provided me daily moments of reflection and insight. I was reminded to slow down and by so doing, it helped me to understand that as a culture, we all deal with a lot of the same challenges, but we can own change and embrace change."

-Brian Luccio,
Sales Executive

"*Journey in the Present* spoke to me in the most raw, authentic way and created a deep yearning for soul-searching to the point that I began reevaluating my values, definition of life success and even future relationships. Tom Matson's gift as a writer is in his ability to draw the reader into his authentic stories in a way that allows them to move out of their current mindful state and move forward in life in a more healthy and positive way."

-Ramon Hill,
Leadership Development Consultant

"*Journey in the Present* was unlike any book I have ever read, and I found myself thinking about Tom's words and introducing conversations with loved ones about all that I processing and feeling. The beauty of Tom's writing is in his questions. How many (authors or books) ask you vs. tell you? I was left processing relationships and opportunities in my future aligned with my values and less about others' approval."

-Kristen Brunkow,
Young Professional

"Tom's thought-provoking chapters made me evaluate how I choose to live my life. The way he speaks from his heart is refreshing and grabbed my attention throughout the book."

-Gabriel O'Shea,
Executive Director

"Rarely does someone come along like Tom Matson, who has seen one of the greatest challenges life can offer and taken that opportunity to discern heartfelt, and meaningful reflections for the benefit of others."

-Greg Harbaugh,
NASA Astronaut (retired)

JOURNEY
IN THE PRESENT

JOURNEY
IN THE PRESENT

Thirty Days to a Thriving, Mindful Life

By

TOM MATSON

MCP, Maitland, FL

Mill City Press, Inc.
2301 Lucien Way #415
Maitland, FL 32751
407·339·4217
www.millcitypublishing.com

ISBN-13: 978-1-63505-449-1
LCCN: 2016915259

Printed in the United States of America

Dedicated to my friend Dr. Shane Lopez.
The day I was told that I had lost my hearing in
my left ear and that my balance would never come
back, I called Shane and he lovingly reminded me to
believe in a future that is better than the present. His
voice was encouraging and tender, and he spent the
next hour asking me hope-filled questions that
showed me I had the power
to make it so.

CONTENTS

CONTENTS CONT'D

AUTHOR'S NOTE

Years ago, through an MRI, I discovered that I'd been given the gift of a brain tumor. Rather than allowing others to "do life" with me during that time, I went into my head. Needless to say, words were hard to come by — so much so that I used my first book, *Unfrozen*, as a way to share my journey.

While it was a brain tumor that changed things in my life, I do not by any means think my life changes are better or worse than yours. We all have our "stuff," and we get to decide how we respond to the hand we've been dealt.

This book was written in the hope that your mindset will be one of growth, and that you will stretch and soak up a new perspective as you not only profess your values, but own them and align your life with them.

In honor of Prince, a fellow Minnesotan who passed away in 2016:

"Dearly beloved, we are gathered here today to get through this thing called life...."

May your life be lived to the fullest, and may your legacy be aligned with your thriving, values-based lens.

All net proceeds from *Journey in the Present* go to brain tumor & epilepsy research.

DAY 1: SLOW DOWN

I'm too busy. You're too busy. We are all too busy! I spent the last month doing my own Gallup poll, and when I asked people "How are you?" I listened for the most common response. One word won by a majority: "busy." I heard about how late you've been working. I heard about how many activities your kids are involved in. I heard about the trips you have been on for work and for fun. I heard about the boards you serve on, and I heard you explain how your life feels out of control.

You do realize that these are choices you've made, right? Every single day, you can wake up and choose to let the world control you, or you can choose to make positive decisions. Plan your schedule wisely and prioritize health, balance and a calmer mindset.

Have you ever really dug into the meaning of the word "busy"? In Chinese, the word consists of two syllables, one meaning heart and the other death.

The busier we become, the more energy flows to the head and away from the heart.

The busier we become, the more we tend to distance ourselves from others and their emotions.

The busier we become, the more selfish we are toward others. We get lost in the chaos and only talk about our needs, our lives and ourselves. You see, even when you respond graciously and ask, "And how are you?" I notice that your phone is still out and buzzing. I notice that you are looking around at other people, or checking the door to see whom you might run into. I notice you checking your watch, and if

1

I talk slowly, I notice your attempt to speed up our conversation. How do I notice these things? Because I used to rely on those same tricks, and I still fall into the habit of them from time to time.

And sadly, our addiction to busyness keeps us from ever asking why. The less we look into our hearts and reflect, the more we remove ourselves from our authentic purpose.

How does your busyness communicate to others what you value? Are your values in alignment with where you put your time, energy, money and emotions?

DAY 2: CARPE DIEM

Well, I did it. I'm "that" guy. Maybe it was a midlife crisis, but I sure hope not. I hope that it was something bigger than my version of a red sports car.

Early last summer, shortly after Morgan graduated from high school, the two of us went out to lunch. I've gone through life thinking that the best restaurants in the Twin Cities are at least 20-30 minutes away from wherever I am at the moment. In reality, I'm not entirely convinced of this, but I do think that an hour of driving with the radio off and with my loved ones by my side is precious, and I wouldn't trade it for anything. It's pure, quality, uninterrupted time that is simply a gift to the soul. Of course, it doesn't always work exactly right. You see, Tyler would get distracted by his phone (and his surroundings, for that matter) if I were driving. And if he were driving? Well, that's a different story. When Tyler drives, he just talks. About what? It doesn't actually matter to me. All I know is that a 16-year-old who loves to talk to his dad is a blessing.

Please understand one more thing. If there are more than two of us in the car, the dynamics change. The tension increases naturally, and the pace of the conversation feels different to me. So, my "drive with the radio off" theory has a clause to it: "Drive with the radio off *if* there are fewer than three people in the car."

Since I was just with Morgan that day, my theory was in full swing, and we set off for the restaurant. I began asking the open-ended questions that my kids have grown accustomed to, and the drive started out like any other. In fact, it's all my kids have ever known, so for them, such questions are expected. With that said, you can start these traditions and patterns on any day of the week, at any point in your life. Just give those who are adjusting to the change time to catch up with you. On this particular drive, I was interested in how Morgan felt about this first summer post-high school.

"Morgan, if I were to watch your friends this summer — and not in some awkward, creepy way — what would I see?"

"Hmm," Morgan hesitated. "Well, you would see more drinking, more smoking pot and more exploring."

"Exploring. Interesting word choice. Can you expand on that?"

She laughed and said, "Dad, I think people are just trying new things more than they used to, but I'm not. That's not where I'm at today, but it does look fun."

"I can see why it looks fun, Mo, and life can be about exploring and seeing new things. But, instead of those things your friends are doing, I wonder how we can find a way for you to scratch that 'wild itch' you are feeling?"

She agreed to think more about it, and she did for a week or so. When she came back to me, she explained that she had just reread my first book about my brain tumor and my journey toward recovery, and how the phrase "Carpe Diem" was woven into the text. Since then, the spirit of that phrase has been woven into my entire life, and Morgan wanted to honor that moment in time for our family.

She asked me whether I had ever truly studied "Carpe Diem," and when I explained what I knew, she shared the following with me:

"In Horace, the phrase is part of the longer 'carpe diem, quam minimum credula postero,' which can be translated as 'Seize the day, put very little trust in tomorrow (the future).' The ode says that the future is unforeseen, and that one should not leave future happenings to chance, but rather, one should do all one can today to improve one's future. This phrase is usually understood against Horace's Epicurean background. The meaning of 'Carpe Diem' as used by Horace is not to ignore the future, but rather not to trust that everything is going to fall into place for you. It's about taking action for the future today."

Morgan looked at me with those amazing blue eyes and said, "Dad, I want to do something to celebrate life. I want to do something to celebrate the chance to seize the day. I want to remind myself each day to make my future better than today. That brain tumor changed not just your life, but all of our lives — and for the better."

At this point, the tears were flowing. I leaned in to hug my beautiful daughter and soak up this perfect gift of a moment, and Morgan timed her words perfectly. "So I want to get 'Carpe Diem' as a tattoo," she said.

"A what?" I asked. *A tattoo*, I thought. Gosh, it could be way worse. She could have wanted to get drunk, high and follow the modern-day version of the Grateful Dead. *But bodies change*, I thought. They are like silly putty. No matter how much I work out and eat right, my former tennis body is more like a lava lamp today, with far more movement than I ever knew was possible. But Morgan had thought about it, and shared that she wanted the tattoo on her foot so that she could wear socks or shoes over it and still look professional. Well, this didn't sound too bad at all! No, this wasn't a bad way to scratch that itch. But then Morgan said, "And Dad, I thought that if I was going to get one, you could get one with me so we can feel that connection forever."

Well, I started crying at that moment. I was so appreciative of my tenderhearted kiddo as I processed whether I could handle the pain of a tattoo. But it was more than that....

Was I too old for a tattoo? Would I faint when I got it? Would I throw up? I tend to start gagging pretty easily, so maybe the pain would be too much for me. Would I cry? That wouldn't be cool.

But who was I kidding? If someone you love deeply wants to share something with you, and it doesn't conflict with your values, you go for it — right? SEIZE THE DAY! So in July, we got our tattoos, mine on my inner wrist and Morgan's on her foot. Did it hurt? Imagine a burning needle going through your skin over and over again. Yes, it hurt! We didn't say a thing the entire ride home, as we were focused on coming down from our adrenaline rush. Do I regret the tattoo? Not for a second. Every single day, I look at my wrist and remind myself to live fully.

What can you do today to do the same? To live fully and completely! What in your life do you hope to change? How can you spark change today and create a future that is more aligned with who you are? Carpe Diem!

DAY 3: BE PRESENT

It's 6:30 a.m., and I'm sitting at the airport eating break-fast. My flight isn't until 11:30 a.m., so why am I here so early? Because my son Tyler loves to drive me. Can you believe that? My 16-year-old son loves waking up at 5 a.m. and driving me to the airport. While I usually love our drive and our time together, this morning was a bit rough, and I'm not the proudest I've ever been as a dad in terms of how I behaved today. You see, I was cold when my alarm went off at 5 a.m., so I got up to prepare my stovetop espresso pot. I wanted the perfect cup of java to start the day off just right. Let's be honest right now — a great day and a great cup of coffee go hand-in-hand. Yet, in addition to an amazing cup of coffee, most great days include long, hot showers as well. This was when my day went south. When I got in the shower, I turned on that perfect hot water, and it came out ice cold. I had to shave, so I showered as quickly as possible, but I still couldn't feel my body. At least I had my coffee waiting for me. *That would make it all better*, I thought, until I realized that I'd forgotten to turn on the burner and didn't have time to prepare my brew before I left. So, that's the person poor Tyler got into the car with this morning... the guy with the cold shower, nicked face and *no coffee*.

As he drove me to the airport at the crack of dawn, Tyler had to listen to things like:

"Tyler, see that car about a mile up there? You should watch that."

"Tyler, how fast are you going?"

"I wonder why you are so quiet today."

7

"You excited about your shower when you get home?"

Here I was, so excited to have that quality time with him, and I'd already let my day take over at 6:30 a.m. My day won over my attitude. I wish I could blame the situation on my lack of coffee, but in reality, those days happen. They don't always come together the way we want them to. But we all need to cut ourselves some slack. We need to remind ourselves that we are human, and that we should never, ever — not even for a second — stop trying.

While I was writing to you and beating myself up, I just watched a father sit down with his son as the dad played on his phone. Ironically, the son did the same. They didn't say anything for the 30 minutes that I watched them. I wondered whether that dad ever thinks about what he is communicating to his son? I wonder if that son thinks that the people on the other end of the phone are more important to his dad than he is? I wonder how the father's actions will teach the son to communicate in the future, and whether he will have the communication skills he needs to drive conversations?

What would it communicate to others if we put our phones away in their company? I wonder how contagious it would be, and what it would do to their life patterns. So, following my cold shower and nonexistent coffee, I had the gift of quality time with a loved one, and though I was obnoxious, self-centered and critical, it was still a gift. I doubt that Tyler will remember it in the future, but if he does, I will own it and laugh about the experience, and I will attempt to teach him to do the same.

I still have another five hours before my flight for that chance to be present with my son. Would I leave that early in the morning and make that same choice again? In a second. Did my hope for quality time and closeness work this time? No, it did not. Did Tyler deserve an apology? He sure did, and he got one. I owned my lens and asked for a snooze that day.

A chance to start fresh. Of course, the good part of the day has yet to come, and the same applies to you and your day.

Could you put your phone down today and walk away from it? Life will go on. Could you arrange your chair so that you are facing the person you are talking to and look them in the eyes as you speak? Who do you need to apologize to today, and how could you have done a better job of owning things?

DAY 4: FEEDBACK

How can we give feedback on behaviors without knowing others' value systems?

We live in a culture that proclaims, "Feedback is a gift." But is it really? As my kids and friends would share with you, I seek feedback on a regular basis. Heck, I seek feedback on the feedback I give. But do I really know enough about a person to provide fair and healthy feedback? Often, my feedback refers to observable behaviors and/or patterns in another person. In theory, this makes sense for the people I truly know — for those whom I've taken the time to truly understand. But what about those outside of my inner circle? When we give others feedback on just behaviors, it does not honor who they are. In fact, our feedback may be more about our needs than theirs.

In order to give appropriate feedback, we need to compare the receiver's actions with their values. Values are the map, and others' behaviors are either in alignment with those values or not.

It's like tracking your spending, but not having a guide to know whether you are going over your budget.

With behavior, we have to start by listing values, then laying out goals and hopes, and then — and only then — can we give feedback on others' behavior.

If someone drank too much, smoked too much and stayed out too late, our mistake would be to give them feedback without first taking the time to know what value system they proclaim. Maybe those choices *are* what they value. Maybe they do live life fully, day after day, and it's the social side of all those things that they value. Though I may disagree with their choices, if their decisions are in alignment with their values and they are aware of them, who am I to judge or give feedback?

The same thing applies to black and white thinkers regarding politics, religion, etc. If they choose to judge, only hang out with those who are similar to them and vote for the same party every year without researching all the candidates — and yet these things are in alignment with their values — who am I to give feedback on their actions? I might deeply disagree with their values, and I may choose not to connect with them. But that's a values-based decision.

Do you know what those around you truly value? Have you taken the time to ask and listen? Do you know what you truly value and what guides your behaviors? If you don't know others' values, ask. And if you don't know your own? Dig in and process.

DAY 5: WHICH BRAIN?

Y ears ago, scientists and doctors assumed that when our brain wasn't in active talking/learning/reading mode, it was at rest. In reality, the opposite is true. The brain isn't at rest; rather, it's in what we now call our default mode. And default mode is where our brain spends half the day. Ironically, default mode is not our brain at rest. In fact, scientists have found that this mode can be quite negative and focused on the self. According to the Mayo Clinic, our default brain encourages us to create non-truths in our minds, making up imaginary "what ifs," engaging in the directionless, pulling what feels like related facts from different times periods and talking *at* people rather than *with* them. It's a shallow, self-centered brain mode.

However, our default brain mode can be balanced by the rested, healthy brain. This second state debates the rationale of our default brain. Not only is it the brain mode that reminds us to be rational, but it allows for a calmer mind and a thriving self.

However, in order to achieve that balance, the brain needs to be rested (through sleep, alone time, reflection and meditation), fed healthfully (wholesome brain food, water, little to no coffee and little to no alcohol) and stimulated by the right inputs (i.e., our social needs are met and balanced). Our hearts should be worked in a healthy way as well (through exercise and by having healthy people around us to make our hearts better). If any of these things begin to spiral out of control, our default brain mode wins, and observable behaviors, word choices, contagious attitudes and actions for others to see shift as a result. For example, the outcomes of our life's work shift (our grades and work performance suffer), our relationships shift (we focus on the negative, gossip more and play into drama), our health shifts (we gain weight or lose too much weight, get sick and sleep less) and finally, we attempt to control the wrong things instead of addressing the right things (meaning the things that truly require our attention). So, unless we slow down and gain self-awareness — unless we make bold changes — it's a slippery slope that lets our default mind win.

What is your current brain mode? What's your lens on life today? How can you change your lens in a healthy, effective way?

DAY 6: I'M SORRY

I heard those words last night, and maybe you have recently as well? For some reason, those two words did nothing to alleviate the tension. In fact, to be honest, I feel more irritated today than I did yesterday in the midst of all the conflict. While the conversation didn't go exactly as follows, this is what it felt like:

"Tom, I'm sorry that you thought I was calling you a jerk."

"I didn't feel like you were calling me a jerk," I replied. "Rather, that's what you literally called me."

"Well, I didn't mean for it to come out like that, so I'm sorry you took it that way."

"Hmm. Well, how else could you have meant it?"

"Well, I would never want you to think you are a jerk. So that wasn't my intention at all."

"Yeah, I'm still missing how else I could have interpreted what you said?"

"Well, I'm sorry you felt upset."

"I'm still struggling to understand what exactly you are apologizing for. I hear the words communicating that you are sorry, and yet it feels like it's all on me. How I interrupted it, how I responded emotionally, etc."

I wonder what the words "I'm sorry" really mean? I use them often. We all do, in fact — or at least we all should if we are genuinely sorry. But the meaning of these words? Well, their meaning is open to interpretation, and that's where the challenge lies. When we communicate words that we believe mean one thing, and the receiver perceives them to mean another, our communication breaks down. Suddenly, words that were meant to create healing create tension instead. Suddenly, words we intended to be loving become painful for the other person.

For some of us, "I'm sorry" is a way of saying "I don't want to talk about this anymore." If I'm candid, it's a way of saying "Will you shut up about (the topic)?" It may not be that you don't want to talk about it (or maybe you truly don't), but that you don't think you want to talk about it with the current emotional charge you are feeling. There is just something about those emotions that shuts us down. Some of us feel them at our core, and they are so overwhelming that we have a hard time speaking. When we free ourselves from those emotions that hang heavy upon our hearts, we will be ready to talk. But not right away.

Is that pattern healthy? Sure it is... *if* you respect the other person enough to finish the conversation. If we simply apologize to end the conversation and never come back to it, well, that's not healthy for anyone. You see, you have a voice that deserves to be heard, and you have ears that deserve to truly listen to what others have to say. Communication needs to flow both ways, and if you have the courage to share your views, then you are also courageous enough to accept others' views on the same topic.

Sometimes saying "I'm sorry" is perfectly timed and the right thing to say. It provides healing, calms the other person's soul and allows you to talk about what really matters in that specific moment in time. So for you, it's not the apology that leads to a healthy or broken conversation; rather, it's the message that follows the apology. If we go from sincerely apologizing to defending our actions, well, that feels different.

Instead of jumping the gun and saying you are sorry too soon, I wonder how we can truly own our actions. Without casting blame. Without deflecting. Without bailing on the conversation, but truly and authentically owning our actions.

The next time you feel relational tension or make a mistake, think about how you can truly own it. How can you own the situation in a way that prompts healthy closure and honors the other person? You can't own how they choose to respond to you, but you can own your actions, your communication and your apology. And maybe, just maybe, they will learn from you like you've learned from them. Now *that's* healthy communication.

DAY 7: CHANGING ROLES

How does your role with your child, parent or friend differ from the roles that others play? Are you open to changing your role?

I always consider how the role I play in the lives of my loved ones differs from the roles their friends and family members play in their lives. When we have a limited amount of time with them, the depth of our connection has to be deeper than ever, and as such, we need to know what we truly desire in our time together. While shared experience is a gift, shared experience with depth in conversation is impactful and potentially life-changing.

I always consider this when I spend time with my kids. They can share meaningful experiences with many people, and because of that, I can't think for a second that I'm the only one creating meaningful shared experiences with them. But I can — and should — consider how my time with them is different from my time with others? The difference is in the conversation and the depth of our connection. The reality is that my children can have great conversations with others too.

So, how can you be different, bolder, deeper and more impactful while still honoring them and the role they want you to play? We don't want to be just another friend; our children want the role we play to feel different. Instead of going to a movie, can you go for a walk and model healthy actions with great questions that allow your relationship to grow deeper? Can you prepare dinner with them and weave in great conversation in the midst of all the slicing and dicing? Such decisions allow us to learn more about our loved ones, and we can't assume we know the role they want us to play (or even that they want us to play the same role we have always played).

My daughter Morgan is now thriving in college. She is changing, just as she should be. She is growing and understanding the meaning of independence. If I try to play the same role in her life that I did when she was in high school, I wouldn't be honoring her. If I'm candid, I don't know what role we are playing in each other's lives at the moment, as our old family dynamics have shifted. I used to know my role and its uniqueness. That said, Morgan has done an amazing job of opening up to others and creating depth. And that leaves me with a choice. I can be like her friends, or I can choose to change. I can ask about how her conversations feel with others. About the people she shares her heart with. Who she is vulnerable with. It allows me to see how she is trusting and letting others in, and it also allows me to find a way to be unique and let others take on the role I used to play. It allows me to adjust.

We need to ask our loved ones what roles they play within the family. What roles they own in terms of dynamics. How else can we give them feedback on how they are communicating if we don't know what role they believe they play?

We also need to consider (and help our loved ones consider) what happens when they can no longer play the role they are used to. We all go through hard times, and we want our children to know that they will change roles, and that it's okay to do so. That's what happens when we grow up and change.

Consider asking them how they will play their role when they are sad or struggling in life? Will they know how to take on new roles in the lives of their friends and family?

Such questions allow them to think about their impact on family dynamics. It's also feedback for them if ever they claim a role and then stop playing it. Not only do these questions affirm the role that they currently play, but they allow your children to ask, "How does it feel to have to play that role? What will it feel like when we can't? How will we communicate when we can't?"

Whether in our marriage, friendships or relationships with our parents or kids, we need to understand what role our loved ones are attempting to play in our lives, and they need to know what hopes you have for their role. Conversations where both parties are open and willing to meet halfway are key. If your aging parents assume your role is to visit them every day, and you can't manage that, how can you navigate the situation with others' support? Friends, siblings and other relatives can help. When we hope for changes in others, we need to know that dynamics will change. There may be natural, healthy tension involved, and even that's okay (and again, healthy). A growth lens on our relationships is one we can never stop talking about, for we know we must ask about and listen for change. How are those around you changing? How are their roles shifting and their values evolving? If you don't know, ask.

DAY 8: WORDS

No matter how quiet or talkative people are, everyone has words they desire and deserve to hear. Words that encourage us, challenge us and show us love. Words that hold us accountable and keep us on the right path. Bluntly said, words matter, and so does our intent. But in a world of instant communication where we can so quickly and flippantly respond to others, I think that many of us forget about the damage our words can cause. Are we using our words in an emotional response, or for the purpose and growth of others? What is our intent?

My challenge is that I often create things in my mind that I don't know to be true. This tends to happen when I'm tired and moving too fast in life. When I am struggling with my well-being, the stories I create in my mind struggle as well. There were years when I would make up stories and then attempt to communicate boldly about what I thought I had heard. In fact, I used to debate from this lens. I would use words based on the story in my mind instead of asking questions to clarify whether the things I saw were true. There is no other way to say it... this was a selfish communication style at best. I would assume I knew *why* you were doing what you were doing. I would assume I knew what was behind your actions. I had to learn to ask myself, *Do you know that to be true, or are you creating it in your mind?* It's such a basic question, and yet it forced me to slow down enough to determine whether I knew the answer.

Though I may seem like I have figured out how to slow myself (and my words) down, in reality I haven't. I have actually had to create a second "layer of defense" to slow my patterns. I love words so much that I use them very quickly, which is why email and texting are dangerous for me. So, if I ask myself whether I know what I'm thinking to be true and then ignore the answer, I've learned that I need to keep my quick-moving mind in check. How do I manage that? I write to myself. I have an app on my phone that I use for journaling — let's call it "Tom's dysfunctional lies he created in his mind." Before I send a text to someone who is laced with emotions, I write exactly what I want to say in that journal and then walk away. Often, in that moment in time, we aren't talking about urgent communication; rather, we're simply talking about communication entwined with high levels of emotion. So I write and write and write, and then set my phone down and walk away. Sometimes for an hour, but if I'm truly attempting to be healthy, I walk away for longer than that.

When I come back to my phone after that break — after taking the time to breathe deeply, walk and rest — I reread what I wrote, and 99% of the time I delete it. Why? Because it was simply a dysfunctional thought process. My words were self-serving at best. They were irrational, attacking and sometimes rude. If I'd sent them out, I would have damaged others and myself. When we feel the need to attack, call someone out and fall into poor communication patterns, we really ought to slow ourselves down. We need to ask ourselves hard questions. We need to write and then delete what we've written. We need to take care of ourselves.

How can you slow yourself down before you respond to someone? What mechanisms will allow you to keep your words in check? How can you still get your words out without causing damage by having others read them? Your words matter.

DAY 9: LIFE AUTHORSHIP

Invictus

By William Ernest Henley

Out of the night that covers me,
Black as the pit from pole to pole,
I thank whatever gods may be
For my unconquerable soul.
In the fell clutch of circumstance
I have not winced nor cried aloud.
Under the bludgeonings of chance
My head is bloody, but unbowed.
Beyond this place of wrath and tears
Looms but the Horror of the shade,
And yet the menace of the years
Finds and shall find me unafraid.
It matters not how strait the gate,
How charged with punishments the scroll,
I am the master of my fate,
I am the captain of my soul.

We are the authors of our story. Yet, many go through life believing they are not, and they become characters in someone else's story rather than their own. Remember that you are the captain of your soul — and I know it's not always easy. Sometimes it's easier to blame other captains, or to ask for a break from charting the course of your ship. It takes years to determine whether post-brain tumor radiation works for the patient. The number of people who have asked me, "Aren't you glad to have that behind you?" is more than I can count. You don't want to fall into a pattern of correcting people you don't know very well, so I would simply smile and say, "I sure am." But as life went on, challenges linked to my procedure caught up with me. Over time I developed epilepsy, and it took months before I became aware of what was happening. It felt like sledding in slow motion with all of my friends running up and down the hill, taking multiple trips while I was still on my first one.

When I say "over time," I mean years. It felt like my life was stuck in slow motion, moving much more slowly than I was used to. I went from someone who took pride in my ability to multitask to constantly losing track of what others were saying. I'd sit in meetings with a ringing ear, completely unable to focus. In fact, the same thing would occur while speaking in front of thousands of people. Eventually, I found out that I was having a series of mini-seizures throughout the day. These seizures were keeping me from reaching a healthy REM state of sleep. I would check out for roughly 10 seconds at a time, and I would be completely unaware of it. My health was killing my ability to focus, and I struggled to think and do what I was paid to do.

It would have been easy to grow angry at life. To become a victim and look at life through a broken lens. Never in my life have I felt more out of control, insecure and fearful as I did then. I wonder what it was like for my loved ones at the time? I suspect I seemed inconsistent, and I also bet that they were fearful of the man stumbling around them. But then, we all have our "stuff." Each and every one one of us has our challenges. Divorce, weight issues, learning disabilities, lost friendships, infertility, cancer, MS — the list goes on and on.

Each and every one of us experiences pain, challenges, fear and insecurity. What differentiates us from others in this thing called life isn't our points of pain, but our ability to find the good in the midst of trouble. Our ability to recover, adjust our lives and embrace the future. We need to walk around with our heads up and see the beauty around us. We need to listen to others' stories. We need to find the good while still honoring our emotions. Remember, you are the captain of your ship.

What path will you take? What can you do today to see the good in your life? What can you do today to take a small step toward seeing others, and not just looking at yourself in the mirror? Life isn't easy, and yet today is a new day. How can we encourage, celebrate and impact? You are the captain of your soul.

DAY 10: WHO YOU ARE

W ho are we? Are we what we do, how we dress and what we show others? In conversations, are we constantly talking about ourselves in order to validate our role as a parent, friend or worker?

The challenge with these behaviors is that when those things are removed, we don't know who we are. We become lost. Remove the "thing" that we believe identifies us, and suddenly there is an emptiness that we don't know how to fill. It's in these moments that we can fall into habits that will damage our long-term well-being. We overspend, overdrink, talk too much about ourselves and work out too much in order to look better, and then tell others about it. We attempt to fill that void with temporary happiness. And temporary happiness is not true happiness.

When I was on the road speaking every weekend, I began to identify myself as a speaker. I would tell everyone I met about my travels, about how many people I spoke to and how far in advance I was booked. And looking back, I would guess that 90% of my conversations began with the word "I." Yet, when I discovered that my speaking limited my ability to be present in the "real world," and that it was hurting my overall health, I stopped. And the thing was, when I stopped, conversations became a challenge and I no longer knew what to talk about. You see, when I removed my identity as a speaker without any comfort in who I was, I was lost. I just didn't know it at the time, but gosh, I felt it at the core of my being. It felt like a midlife crisis, and I wanted to buy things to fill that void. Actually, that's what many people do, and that's exactly what I did. When people remove that outside approval mechanism without knowing who they are, they go above and beyond to show off their success. They buy new clothes (I did), they buy new cars (I did), they spend too much on their house and they begin to talk about themselves even more. They will do anything to show off their success.

What a lonely world to chase. A world spent chasing others' approval. A world where you lose your identity if you are let go from your job. A world where you no longer have a purpose when your kids go off to college. A world where your image is your most prized possession.

If we get fired tomorrow and move into smaller homes, and if our kids and spouse leave the house, then the impact of these changes will be very different if we truly know ourselves and our values. Now, of course we would feel sad, but these things wouldn't change how we view ourselves. What we do is not who we are. Your house doesn't show who you are. Your style of dress doesn't show who you are, and neither do the people you date. Bluntly and playfully said, no one cares about those things, and you shouldn't either. It doesn't matter where you live (as long as you're safe), nor does it matter what your kitchen countertop looks like or what kind of car you drive, or even how many friends you have. If these things matter (too much) to you, you need to hold up a mirror and look inward. You need to figure out what void you are trying to fill.

Life is about being authentic and comfortable in our skin. It is about loving ourselves as we are. Do you love yourself the way you are? Can you talk about yourself without telling others what you do that makes you great? Do you love and accept the real you? If not, spend some time journaling and thinking about the real you and the core values that define you. You are beautiful as is, but you need to believe that and quit seeking outside approval. Love yourself today because you are worth it. You are a gift.

DAY 11: HIGHS AND LOWS

I t's been one of those years for me, and it's a year I know many of you have felt as well. (Maybe you are feeling it today.) The kind of year where the pain overwhelms the soul. Whether the loss of my loving aunt, the pain of friends mourning the loss of their young son, a friend mourning the loss of her spouse or the struggles of those who lost their jobs or marriages, it's a year that I'm ready to have in my rearview mirror.

In all instances, I thought about how in the valleys of life, we search for anything and everything that will give us calm in the eye of the storm. We want our pain to be removed and fixed. I think the personal challenge is that in times of suffering, our pain keeps us from looking inward, and instead we search for answers to the larger questions in life that permeate our minds during sleepless nights. This year, I've been searching for the profound answer to that lifelong question... where is God in the midst of pain? I have also been exploring the deeper question of why God won't make others' pain go away? This was my attempt to respond to all my loved ones who have been searching for the answer to those questions.

Good morning, my friend. I'm sure you are working today and attempting to fake life/work presence, when in reality, it's often such a foreign place to be. A life disconnect, so to speak. With that said, my hope for you today will be small glimpses of the perfect questions or beauty in the day you didn't expect. Often, when we are internal, we literally and figuratively turn inward and stop looking up and noticing the beauty around us. So, to start, this is my subtle nudge to put that head up today as you look into the sky. Look into others' eyes, knowing they too have pain/feelings they are carrying with them today, and simply allow yourself to take a deep breath. In the midst of pain, we often feel so deeply alone, but life goes on and others are feeling similar pain. And if we all put our heads up and look into each other's eyes as we walk, then maybe, just maybe we will remind them (and they us) that we aren't alone on this life journey.

With your question about God's peace/presence, you know that I just can't give you a cliché answer, but as a non-pastor/non-counselor, I'll do my best to respond lovingly and authentically. To begin, as you process this question with others, know that some won't know how to respond and in fact won't respond. It will push them too far away from their views of a loving faith alone and talking about your pain and anger will make them uncomfortable. That is their choice to make, and yet to me, that puts God into a safe box that sadly hinders the bigness of God. As I view my own faith, I believe we get to see a full glimpse of God by soaking up the good and the bad in life, and not just views or readings that make us feel good 24/7. When we take a step back and look at life, it's messy and full of raw emotion. It can look and feel like a reality TV show (one that may be on later in the evening). Life is filled with pain, sadness, hurt, anger and more. I believe that across the globe, God is viewed as one who understands suffering just as much as love and peace. In my study of Positive Psychology, I think others in my profession would agree with owning and allowing ourselves to feel pain and suffering because they are real, authentic and involve real life, which allows us to know and feel God's presence. Whatever your views on faith, I truly believe that God gave you anger and sadness just as much as happiness. They are equally valued and equally about healing.

Finally, if we choose to believe in God and we want to see glimpses of God daily, then we need to be open enough to search for and accept God in anger, sadness and hurt just as much as we rejoice in God in moments of love, grace and peace. So my friend, my takeaway is that closeness to God is in our vulnerability and authenticity. It is in being true to what you feel. If you are angry, be angry. If you are hurt, be hurt. But please don't run from pain due to the fear of feeling it. Too often we want to hide from pain because it's unbearable, but instead of hiding from it (as it will come out later in a different, often dysfunctional way), honor it and let yourself feel it. We can't know love without truly living and knowing pain. We can't know ourselves either. Those who survive the pain of cancer, the loss of a child or other family members and more are richer because of it, not because of the cliché reason why, but because they allowed themselves to feel it. By surviving this, life is about to get a whole lot richer, but honor that heart and those feelings for today. God is in the midst of them, and those who love you are too. Your true friends and family will be there in your messiness, and you will remain lovable, safe and beautiful to us all. You are a gift, and we will all learn from this chapter in your journey. It will change you, and let it. However it does, we will all be right there.

All my love,
Tom

DAY 12: UNBALANCED

I s work your number one value? Do you prioritize your work over your other values? Though I certainly don't mean to, I often communicate that to my loved ones. I beyond love what I do, but you see, work isn't my top value — and yet I tend to schedule my life like it is. I non-verbally communicate its priority without reflecting on what that means for the people I love and care for. I've been talking to friends this past month, and I've found that many do the same. We schedule every month around our work, and by so doing, we are communicating to ourselves that work wins, and that it's our key value.

Why do we do this? Have you truly thought about it? Sometimes I wonder if my identity and self-worth are more wrapped up in what I do than I care to admit. But today I'd like to change my lens on life, and I encourage you to do the same.

Work can't be the only recipient of your time and energy, for when that happens, we sacrifice other values and often give up the things that truly give us life. You need to schedule your time in a way that improves your well-being, so don't fall into the trap of prioritizing work above everything else.

For me, when work wins and I fall short in the other areas of my life, my reaction to the world starts to change. I find myself more irrational, less kind, less patient and I tend to shut down much more quickly than I would otherwise. My emotions and stress start sneaking out sideways, and suddenly, spilled milk feels like the world has come to an end.

While we can feel our extreme emotions, understanding why they have shifted is often a challenge. Are you aware enough to know your emotions are coming out in unhealthy ways? How can you slow that train before it becomes a runaway? Can you stop and journal? Can you use a journaling app on your phone to capture your thoughts, and delete them after you reread them in order to intentionally get rid of them?

We watch our focus shift and our mind wander. That's what tends to happen when we don't get enough sleep, eat enough of the right foods and allow our bodies to move and stretch. Can you simply get out and go for a walk each day? When you do, can you leave your phone at home in order to be truly present during your walk? Feel your breath. Appreciate the beauty around you.

DAY 13: CHANGE HAPPENS

Our world is quickly changing, and yet I tend to act shocked every time I see it. It's like I don't know it's coming, and I react with too many emotions, too many words and a lens that is all about me. It feels like falling through the ice, and the second we hit the water, it's like a thousand needles piercing the body all at once. Quick change really is that shocking.

But those reactions to bold change are not what scare me. Rather, it's the small, slow changes. These changes move at such a slow pace that they catch me off guard. These changes are the ones I need to be more aware of. And I can only become more aware of them by becoming more aware of how I react in the midst of them.

So, the next time you start to feel the small changes, sort how you feel. Soak up your feelings and commit them to memory. Our ability to sense our reactions to the smallest of changes is a reminder of how much we have transformed and grown. We can use these reactions to celebrate how far we've come.

Embrace it. Celebrate it. Feel it. And whatever you do, don't talk yourself out of it. Part of us will always try to talk ourselves out of pain when we can learn the most about ourselves during times of stress. Can you let yourself be present and truly feel what you feel, or do you try to quickly distance yourself from your emotions?

Please don't run from them. Change and pain, big or small, are not bad. They just get a bad reputation.

Accept it. Sort it. Own it. Process it.

When we do, we change. When we do, we gain the resiliency we need to deal with future changes. When we own change and allow ourselves to feel it, it stops coming out sideways and we can put it into words. Life is not meant to be lived alone, and our ability to put our feelings into words matters deeply.

How can you calm yourself the next time you experience changes in your life? How does change help you grow and develop? What kinds of changes make you react the most quickly? Finally, how can you embrace the change that comes today?

DAY 14: LIFE IS GOOD

G osh, we are blessed. And yet, in talking to so many friends, I wonder whether those around me feel the same? There is just something in our human condition that makes us want to share the difficult things in our lives and the drama we feel. But I wonder if we realize how much of our attention is spent on such things? I wonder how much our mind is focused on what's wrong rather than on what's strong? I wish I could take credit for that expression, but my co-worker Brandon used it first, and I love it.

You aren't broken, so stop telling yourself you are. We are all works in progress, but if we focus too much on our brokenness, then that's the person we will begin to show the world. Is that how you want to be known? Is that what you want your loved ones to learn from you?

Now, with that said, please don't think for a second that I want you to pretend to be happy if you are suffering. I want you to be authentic to your mood and honor where you are at, but I am raising several questions here because I don't want you to get stuck in a dark place. So honor your mood, and allow yourself to be vulnerable and authentic, but consider the lens through which you are looking at your life.

Have you considered journaling at night about what went well during the day and what you hope for tomorrow? I've been shocked by the difference doing so has made in my life. Years ago, if you read my journals, you would have thought you were reading the words of a deeply depressed person — and yet I wasn't. I know what situational depression feels like, and I have dealt with that pain before. In fact, I think that's why J.K. Rowling described Dementors as soulless creatures and compared their creation to the darkest time in her life. I, like many of you, have experienced that world, and it's a bottomless pit of pain, tears, numbness and confusion. This lens makes it a struggle to see the hopeful future we search for.

While I have felt that pain, that was not the life lens I was looking through when I wrote in previous journals, although my words might indicate otherwise. It wasn't that I was depressed; rather, I was focused on what was broken in my life. I could only think about what was making me sad and mad, and it spilled over into how I viewed the world and interacted with others.

But since I have shifted my focus to positive journaling and life learning, I've found that I have begun to ask others about their positives as well. I've found that I search for people who want to make a positive impact instead of those who are stuck at a negative place in life. It's also changing how I view myself and how I talk to myself. I used to look in the mirror and focus on what I hated — even on the days when I ate healthy meals, exercised, slept well and had much to rejoice in. By focusing on the good in my life, I am also focusing on the good in who I am.

So, at the end of the day, take a few moments and jot down your thoughts on what you loved and learned. Could you do the same with friends the next time you see them? Ask the same about them and see how it changes the nature of your friendships. Also, take the time to consider what you like about yourself, and write down that long list. Love yourself as you are right now. Take care of yourself. Life is a gift, but sometimes we just need to change our perspective in order to see it.

DAY 15: CLEANSING AND PLANTING

I t's that time of year again... spring. For me, that means walks, tennis and sitting outside to enjoy my coffee.

Spring reminds me of trips to the cabin to get the dock put in and the rush of that cold lake water hitting my skin through the holes in my rubber waders. My grandma would be up there with us, and she was one of those people who made you feel great about whatever you wanted to do or be. She always smiled with her eyes, and those beautiful eyes were full of love. I often spent time alone with her up there, and she was the one who introduced me to the joy of planting flowers and gardens.

To this day, I don't remember the finished product, and in fact, maybe there was no finished product, but my memories of those moments with my grandma were magical. She had a methodical way about her, and everything had its place and a certain series of steps to take. First, she would put on her gardening gloves. I loved the images of bold tomatoes and green beans on the outside of those gloves, and I noticed that for someone who loved to plant so much, they were always perfectly clean. Then, she would hand me my matching set and we would grab our tiny shovels and plant. She wore a giant gardening hat, and we would sit down together and just talk about life. She always stopped to point out the butterflies, always made sure we had fresh lemonade and never corrected the way I liked to garden. I loved those times with her. No phones, no TV, no distractions. Just my grandma and me.

So today, I'm cleaning the old dirt out of my planters and flowerpots, just as she taught me to do. I'm repurposing it around the yard and adding fresh potting soil, and soon I will be planting herbs, veggies and flowers.

Fresh soil. Soil full of nutrients. A foundation of health and growth. The proper starting point for all that I hope to grow. What I'm attempting to grow is in deep alignment with my values.

Yet, instead of finishing the job, I'm sitting here writing to you with dirt beneath my fingernails and the smell of earth on my body. While I was standing on my patio and making sure that everything was set up for a great growing season, I began to wonder why I'd been so intentional about my healthy eating values recently. I also pondered why it so deeply matters for me to share those values with my loved ones. I suppose that that's what my grandma did so many years before, and I suppose that's what we all do with those we love the most.

So today, I'm thinking about the relationships in my life.

Some of you were planted years before, right along-side me, and you have continued to go through life with me. You've been a consistent presence, and no matter how much time goes by between our talks, it feels like we just spoke yesterday. Our connection is simply that natural, and I think a lot of that has to do with how aligned we are from a values perspective.

Some of you came later, and based on who you are as mentors and friends, you have deeply shaped my lens on values and the life I was meant to live. A growth mindset permeates from your being, and no matter what, you have allowed me to process shifts in my values and changes in how I view life. As I navigate how I want to live my life, you have asked how you can help me get there.

I suppose that's the foundation of great relationships. The people who have touched us love us and don't assume that since they knew us once, they still know us today. Rather, they see life as a journey of growth and change, and they allow us to grow and change while still remaining true to who we are.

But sometimes it's just not that easy, is it? Sometimes the relationships that were planted in our lives begin to feel different. Perhaps we are both changing — and there is nothing wrong with this at first. You see, I have many friendships where both of us have changed deeply, and yet we remain gifts in each other's lives. If that's the case, why does it hurt so badly when change takes place in other relationships? Why does it create such a disconnect?

Values. When the values in those we hold most dear change and are no longer in alignment with who we are, we begin to feel a small crack in our relationships. The more time goes by, and the more comfortable we become in our growing selves, the more that small crack begins to feel like a great divide. At one point, the distance simply becomes too great, and we are faced with a painful choice with long-term health consequences. Like the vegetables my grandma taught me to grow, we too need healthy soil, nutrients, water and sun. Simply put, if you have a relationship that is getting in the way of your growth, I encourage you to create closure there.

That one relationship isn't only damaging to your health; it's damaging all of the other flowers that are planted around you. Their roots choke other roots, their damage is contagious and you owe it to yourself and others to move on for the sake of your personal growth. You can't stay stuck. You can't stay frozen. You can't risk hurting others, nor can you risk hurting yourself.

To be the person you want to be, and to live the life you are truly meant to live, you need others around you whose values are aligned with yours, and who seek to grow just like you do. In order to thrive, we need others who have a similar definition of thriving in life. In order to feel the joy we are meant to live, we need to replace — or at least deal with — those weeds and dead soil.

You are meant to shine. You are meant to impact. You are meant to grow. You are meant to thrive. Are you willing to spring clean with me today and think about those you surround yourself with? Who do you need to call and affirm today? Who can you thank for making a difference in your life? Who is keeping you from growing? Who provides you the warmth you love and that you would love more of? Seek, spark action and cleanse. By so doing, you will grow into that beautiful you.

DAY 16: LIFE IS VIVID

" S o coming back from a journey, or after an illness, before habits had spun themselves across the surface, one felt the same unreality, which was so startling; felt something emerge. Life was most vivid then."

- Virginia Woolf, *To the Lighthouse*

The word "crisis" comes from a Greek root meaning "to decide," and when we are faced with challenges to our health, we can choose how to respond. Do we want to fall victim to the hand we've been dealt, or do we want to rise above it and shine?

It has now been three years since the end of my post-brain tumor radiation. As I have shared, cutting off blood to that darn golf ball-sized brain tumor has triggered a number of consequences.

One of them is really throwing me off today. You see, I can't hear in large lecture halls anymore. Many of the things I used to love — live theater, concerts, amazing speakers and more — I can no longer hear out of my left ear. The human brain is so amazing, however, that while trying to figure out why my hearing disappeared so quickly, my mind races to figure out what's wrong. Gosh, isn't that incredible? The brain knows that something isn't working correctly, so it shoots off internal flares to tell us there's a problem. While I appreciate this amazing gift, it doesn't feel very good. In fact, when I attempt to describe it to my friends, I always say that it feels like I'm having a panic attack without the emotions. My brain is racing at a speed of 1,000 miles per hour, and I can't calm it down. How do I stop it? I've tried deep breathing. I've tried to adjust my hearing aid. I've tried everything possible, and so far, I've got nothing.

So, I am left with a choice. Put myself into that situation and deal with the recovery process (which reminds me of my days post-concussion). These days feel lonely to me as I attempt to minimize my exposure to bold sounds, bright lights and seemingly quick movements. In addition, to those around me, my nonverbal cues appear empty at times. I can see in others an expression of concern, and even fear as they look into the eyes of their once-vibrant friend and loved one.

So, my choice? I've stopped going to these events, concerts and plays. I've moved on from those things — things that used to matter to me so deeply — and instead of being angry or sad, I rejoice in the chance to learn new things.

I've taken up hiking and love the feel of a breeze upon my face and the peace that nature gives me. I journal more than ever and have found that my reflection has impacted my ability to create change and avoid falling into negative behavior patterns. I've learned to appreciate yoga, and to listen and observe more.

Life is a choice, and today you are given the choice of what life gives you. A few weeks ago, a former NFL star was shot in a horrible road rage incident. In my area, a 66-year-old teacher was attacked by a student when she confiscated his cell phone last week. Everywhere I look, especially in the news, people are reacting to life in ways that hurt them and the people around them. These choices are contagious and life-altering.

Today, when life challenges you — when you don't feel good, when others' words harm you, when it's raining on a day you hoped would be sunny and when you receive feedback that is hard to process — remember that life goes on. Life is about learning. Life is about choices, and today you can choose to look at life through a lens of peace and beauty.

When life challenges you and you feel anxiety rising up from your core, what will you do? How can you calm yourself? What do you need to stop doing in order to end the crisis? Is there someone you can call whose voice calms your soul? Can you journal, walk away, take a deep breath or simply choose to laugh? The choice is yours.

DAY 17: LIFE'S CURVEBALLS

I used to think I had full control. I was the director of this play called life. Making my chess moves. My career moves. Back then, I could have told you every move I was making and why. I took great pride in writing my life resume. I even knew all the clichés to say to make sure you saw me as values-driven.

"God's in control, not me."

"I'm just along for the ride on this journey called life."

"We are all works in progress."

But I didn't truly believe those things. My moves were calculated and strategic. I prided myself on always being a step ahead of everyone else. Maybe there is a reason why I have very few friends in my life from those early years. Those who I surrounded myself with were there not because their values were aligned with mine, but because I needed them.

I spent a majority of my time living in the future. Where was I going? What was I doing? I was planning my next move. My next career choice. Next, next, next!

I used to claim that mentors were the key to life, and yet even my mentors were chosen based on who they were rather than on their values. What I claimed was mentorship was strategic networking and career advancement.

Then life threw me a curveball, and I had this gift in the form of a brain tumor. That was when my old lens on life shattered to pieces.

I'm not in control of my life; rather, I'm in control of my emotional response to life. I'm in control of the life lens that I choose to look through.

I had to throw away those old life lenses and put on new ones, and as I got used to them, I found that life is beautiful in the present moment.

The friends I have around me today truly know me and are in deep alignment with my values.

My financial planner won't be happy about this, but I spent more money today on shared experiences than I saved for my future wealth. The mentors I have wouldn't impress you by title, but their character would leave you awestruck. Personally, I've turned down jobs that looked impressive on paper because they would have hurt my overall well-being and compromised my values. With all of that said, I still fall each and every day, saying the wrong things at times but owning everything I do.

When you walk, can you keep your head up, look around and soak up who you see? Can you smile at the people in your surroundings? Can you reach out to a friend and thank them for the role they play in your life? Can you journal about the parts of yourself that you love and celebrate?

DAY 18: QUIT RUNNING

D on't overreact (or underreact) to your emotions, and quit running to (or from) them too quickly. Why is that so hard for us?

Sometimes we give our past experiences far too much credit and power over our present. We were hurt in our past, so we assume that we'll spend the rest of our lives feeling that way. However, the truth is that our past is option, not law over our future. The past is there for us to learn more about ourselves, but it does not in any way define us.

How can you allow yourself to feel again? Well, to begin, please don't push your emotions away — but don't rush to follow them either. When you welcome your feelings, they will not control you. So embrace them. Attempt to put them into words. Let them permeate your soul.

On any given day, our emotions come and go, and yet I wonder how often we accept them as truths without fully fleshing them out. Candidly, they may simply be things we have created in our minds.

How can we tell what is true? We ask questions. We clarify. We ask ourselves, "Is what I'm feeling true, or am I simply creating it in my mind?"

Clarify your thoughts until you feel calm and take ownership of your emotions. Make sure to let others accompany you on your life journey. Share with them what you are feeling and how you are reacting to the situation, and ask them for their neutral lens. Then, truly listen to what they have to say. By allowing others to reflect on our actions, we can learn from their guidance.

So how do we know when our hearts are not being honored and understood? We lack peace. We feel "off" in life. Misaligned. So, instead of running away from those emotions, run toward them. Embrace them. Align your heart and seek that peace.

Finally, let's stop talking ourselves out of our emotions. Let's stop convincing ourselves that they aren't real. They *are* real and they are important, so keep honoring your feelings and needs. When you listen to your heart, peace and acceptance come. So, what are you feeling today? Who can you reach out to and share what you are feeling and processing?

DAY 19: YOU CAN'T ALWAYS WIN

If you are consistently living in line with your values, and if your words and actions are aligned, then not everyone will like you.

Take that in. How does it feel? Some of you may read those words and feel comfortable in the emotions they evoke. However, others will read those words and feel their heart begin to race, their spirit growing anxious. "Not like me? How is that possible!? I'm likeable! How could someone not like me!?"

Actually, I suppose you are right. Some of you have an amazing ability to win others over and find a way to align your life with the lives of those around you. But at what cost? Now, that's the harder question. Put simply, are you willing to sacrifice your values for the sake of having others like you?

While I value your gift of being able to win people over, and while I appreciate how naturally you draw others to you, if you are willing to sacrifice those guiding principles that you uphold as your compass for life, I question the integrity in that and I hope that you would ask yourself the same question.

Why do we worry so much about being liked by others? I suppose a part of it stems from insecurity. As we are molding ourselves, we have a higher awareness of how others are responding to us. If we are taking on leadership roles and creating great divides between our roles and our followers... well, we cannot call ourselves leaders if we have no followers.

Yet we keep trying to win others over. In fact, some of us will sacrifice the group for the sake of a few people who don't respond to us the way we want them to. Some of us will read the evaluations of an event we planned and become fixated on the two negative ones. We'll take those evals personally, even though we know that we shouldn't.

Maybe that's something we need to own and understand. It's not about us. Have you considered that? If we tracked those who don't like us and see their patterns in life, we may find that they hate others who are also in alignment with their core values. In fact, their bold response to you and your values actually affirms that you are living authentically.

Living in alignment with your values doesn't mean that everyone will agree with you. In fact, you should be so consistent that some people will react to you poorly because they don't know their own values, or because they simply disagree with yours.

So quit trying to win! You can't. You just can't win everyone over without sacrificing what you hold dear. As author Brene Brown taught us in her book *Daring Greatly*, "Don't try to win over the haters; you are not a jackass whisperer." Ah, now that's bold and simply perfect. Do you really want to win others over when you disagree with their lifestyle? Do you really want others whose values boldly conflict with yours to like you?

Maybe it's not a matter of being liked, but of being respected. Instead of attempting to win the haters over, you might be able to sit down with them and have a real conversation, and perhaps you can come to respect each other's lenses without agreeing completely. Leaders can accomplish a great deal with mutual respect. A world of mutual respect allows us to voice our views, listen and honor others.

Have you considered that the reason others don't like you is because you are fixated on naming your values over and over again, with little desire to hear from the people around you? Have you owned impasses in relationships as you lived with a fixed mindset and viewed the world in black and white? "My way or the highway" is not an honoring lens you use to look at life. So today, when you are thinking about those misaligned relationships and roadblocks, what can you own? What can you own rather than rationalize?

Rationalizing. Some of us get confused about what it truly means to own our thoughts and behavior. We think that if we apologize, and then explain why we do and think what we do, then that's ownership. Well, that's far from the truth. Owning our actions means that we name them for others and apologize for the damage they have caused. We seek feedback on how we could have done things differently so that we can learn in the future and create a stronger bridge in our relationships. We listen and choose to have a growth mindset, and to truly honor others' views.

Today, as you go out into the world, choose to like yourself the way you are. Choose to be proud of your values. Accept that not everyone will like you, and that you won't like everyone around you either. But how can you listen to others' opinions without forming your arguments in your mind while they speak? Who do you need to listen to and show more respect to in your life? How can you come to appreciate your lens on the world and how your values are represented? Furthermore, how can you learn today from those who see the world in a different way than you? Now, that's a world I would love to live in. A world full of listening, respect, questions and a growth mindset. Imagine a world where you, politicians, leaders and everyone else lived by such values. That would surely break down the pain we experience and create a cohesive, respectful world. What a gift that would be.

DAY 20: CHOICES

I'm writing on the plane, sitting next to my son Tyler on the way back from a college visit. I was blown away by the beauty of the campus. It was breathtaking and designed (in theory) for students to be successful at every turn. If you forget your student ID, which opens up the door to your residence hall room (no longer called dorm rooms), no problem — you can simply text your door code. A cold, snowy day? All the sidewalks are heated! Our tour guide mentioned that some students opt to set their laundry outside their door, which they can then pick up washed and folded for their convenience.

If you have had the luxury of visiting college campuses in your adulthood, it's amazing how the memories come flooding back. I remember sitting in front of the washing machine in the laundry room of my dorm, and how confusing it was to see all of those dials. If I hadn't run out of clean boxers, I would have put off laundry day, but it was time. It was my third day in college, and I was breaking my mom's rule about always wearing clean underwear in case I got in a car accident. Finally, a hallmate stuck his head in to say hi, and seeing my bewildered face — white and dark piles… whites in warm… darks in cold — he set me free to work my washing magic.

Nowadays, the residence halls have hardwood floors, wireless Internet and cable TV — a bit different from the 9-inch black and white TV, triple room and communal typewriter that we all shared back in the day. In fact, I still remember meeting my roommate Greggy for the first time. He was in school on a full scholarship, and though he was an academic wiz, he struggled socially. He would sleep on top of the covers in his blue tighty-whities, making strange noises with his lips. He had a pair of faux leather Velcro shoes that he shined every night, and I frequently woke up to Greggy sitting at his desk and staring at me while I slept.

But I survived college and loved my experience. In fact, it was life-changing for me, and most of my best friends came from that experience. While Greggy is no longer in my life, he taught me how to appreciate those who are different from what I am used to. In fact, my talks with Greggy about life and politics molded me. College Tom, Mr. City Boy, met farm kids for the first time. I met students who had been in the bottom half of their class with a 3.8 GPA (with only four in their graduating class!), and I met those with different views on religion, the economy, the Iran-Contra hearings and the Cold War.

My mind developed, my values became more grounded and my lens on my career took shape as I walked the paths that great minds before me had walked.

But how can I help others find their same path? How can I help Tyler find his path, his future home and the place where his journey will continue?

It reminds me of watching planes taking off and landing. If the runway lights had roundabouts and were scattered in abstract order, planes wouldn't be able to take off and land properly. The reason planes are able to take off and land thousands of times a day is that the runway lights at airports are perfectly spaced and perfectly lined up. So, just as an airplane can't take off without all the runway lights in perfect alignment, Tyler can't take the proper steps without figuring out what those runway lights represent for him. What does he value? What does he need?

As we processed his experience, Tyler was able to sort that all the students looked the same. While sitting outside the student union and looking around at the beautiful campus, he saw students who were of the same racial background, wore the same style of clothing and even had similar body types. The school with the perfect grounds, buildings and campus suddenly looked less perfect once we saw past the brick and ivory pillars. Suddenly, the school with the marketing materials that painted a picture of perfection no longer felt so perfect, for the "sameness" of the school was disturbing to Tyler.

Ah, a runway light began to appear. Second, the school lacked something to rally around that would bring the community together — and there it was, another value emerging. As we talked, those runway lights became more and more clear, and we began to align Tyler's hopes, desires and passions with the next steps he would take. Stewardship mattered to him (thank goodness), and so did proximity to family. By asking him the right questions, the end of our talk armed him with an understanding of what he was looking for in a school.

When we search for a career that aligns with our values, we need those same runway lights. Those values that we hold dear should be aligned with our employer's values. Often, we search for jobs and roles rather than corporate values. We ask questions about the salary and daily responsibilities, and we confirm that we understand the reporting structure. However, we often fail to see how organizational values are not simply professed, but embodied in the smallest of ways throughout the company.

Today, as you think about helping others (or yourself) find the right organization, church, synagogue, career or volunteer location, think about those runway lights. What do you desire from a values perspective? What do you need to see in those organizational truths? Is there anyone you can turn to today who is willing to ask those questions and allow you to process your answers? When your values are aligned, you are at your best, and your employer will get the very best out of you.

DAY 21: YOGA AND HIKING

Ten minutes from my house is an old ski area that shut down in the early 1980s. It is now overgrown with trees, and a volunteer group has maintained it as a nature reserve, complete with woodchip-lined hiking trails.

When I first found my hiking hideaway, I would stop and rest halfway through my trek. You are basically walking straight up the ski hill, so I figured that section of the trail was a healthy place to take a short break. But this summer, my mindset changed, and now I slow my pace a bit and make it straight to the top of the hill.

By slowing my pace, I've noticed that I hear and see more. I notice the trees swaying in the wind and the rustling sound of the animals running through the leaves. Plus, that view at the top — it's a majestic view of the river below, and you can see trees for miles around. It takes your breath away, which isn't always a great thing when you are struggling to catch your breath, but it's well worth it.

As Homer reminded us, "The journey is the thing," and as author Dan Eldon declared, "The journey is the destination."

Yet, somehow that message becomes lost as we seek to win and fixate on our own outcomes. That's what I did when I first started yoga. I would watch others and try to do more than they could. I would hold the pose longer. Stretch more. I was so deeply fixated on others that I failed to soak up the gift of yoga in my heart, mind and soul.

One day our instructor said, "Whatever you do is fine. Don't judge it." Don't judge it? I was always judging it.

Comparing it. Trying to beat it and judging myself along the way.

If only I would have...

I should have...

Everyone else has done it....

Maybe that's why decade birthdays are so full of reflection and dread. When we hit those key dates, we find ourselves looking around to see where others are at in their lives. We wonder if we are at the same point in our careers, families, finances and relationships. If we do not like what we find, then we tend to question our place in the world. But that's all the more reason to create your special day the way that you want it to be! Massages, hikes, times with family and friends and perfect moments of laughter are even more vital on such days. Yet sadly, many forget about these moments, and maybe that's why people find those birthdays so depressing

Living in a world of comparison is a lose-lose situation. It makes for a lonely lens because if we win, others must lose. And if we lose? Well, then we sit in that world and play a comparison game, focusing on our lives' points of pain.

Maybe that's why we put our heads down and race up those hills. We begin to view our worth as a race, and we long to have the "best" car or the "best" career.

But this is your path. Your journey. Your destination. No one defines your worth but you. No one defines your life success but you. Today you have the choice to not only accept who you are, but to embrace who you are. This is your chance to live within your means. A chance to celebrate the good in each and every day.

What do you hope for in your journey? How can your day be defined not by what you have or do, but by who you are and how you choose to speak to yourself and others? *Namaste.*

DAY 22: RALLY CAPS

In 1980, our country went through a challenging time. Mortgage interest rates hovered at around 15%. We had oil shortages, rising gas prices and a floundering economy. Polls during that time showed an American voice united in fear, and many predicted a future less hopeful than the present.

Since I was only 10 years old, I didn't feel the angst in my life. I had never grown up with much money, so the visual shifts weren't as bold for me as they were for others. Plus, my loving parents always found ways to get me involved in things. From finding used equipment to borrowing my friends' stuff, I lived in a world of support and community.

Growing up in Minnesota, kids tend to have one sport on the brain, and that's hockey. In the late '70s, the local university had just come off of two straight national championships, but instead of trying to win a third straight, Herb Brooks stepped away to coach the Olympic hockey team.

When Coach Brooks picked his team, he didn't select the best players. Rather, he chose the players who would align with the system he had created. Success wasn't something that the American hockey team was known for in the Olympics, but Brooks wanted to give it a try. Now remember, this was in the midst of the Cold War, and even a 10-year-old like me was in fear of the Soviet Union and the power they professed. This power existed not only in the nuclear arms race, but on the hockey rink as well.

There is no other way to say it — the Russians ruled the world of ice hockey. From a young age, their talents and skills were finely tuned to align with the Soviet hockey system, and watching them skate was like watching an artist at work.

The Russian Olympic team was made up of men who had been playing together for years, and who had achieved nothing short of perfection on the ice. Before 1980, the Russian hockey team had won the gold medal in five of the last six Olympic Games, and they were such a well-oiled machine that they also handedly beat the NHL All-Stars in 1979. Simply put, they were the best of the best, and year after year they have proven this fact to be true.

After all the success Herb Brooks had as a college coach, you would assume that he'd focus on continuing with the same model he had always known. That's what most of us would do, and in fact, that's what many managers tend to do as well. When we get a glimpse into the ego and mindset of a successful coach, you would see most of them falling in love with a system and riding it out through their tenure. We constantly hear of these stories in the NFL and other professional sports, and as a coach, I know how hard it is to be willing to change. But that's the attitude leaders have, and that's the attitude we need to have.

Our mindset needs to be one of betterment. Our life vision has to be aligned with possibility and growth.

So what did Coach Brooks do to prepare to beat the mighty Russians? He brought together a group of teenagers who were willing to play for something bigger than themselves. He put a team around him and asked them to put their egos and individual accolades aside for the sake of the team and the United States of America.

Of course, most of us have seen the movie or read stories about how the United States Olympic ice hockey team beat the Russians in the semifinals of the 1980 Olympic Games in Lake Placid, New York. That team of teenagers went on to win the gold medal.

But it wasn't just hockey enthusiasts from North Dakota, Minnesota, Wisconsin and Massachusetts who rallied behind the team. You see, in the midst of the pain and hopelessness the nation was feeling, we (the United States) needed something to rally around that was bigger than ourselves.

We all know what pain and fear feel like. For me, it was a brain tumor, and for you it might be watching your kids' lives go in an unexpected direction. Maybe it's the pain you carry over a failed relationship. Of course, your pain doesn't have to be about people — it could be the result of a layoff, your parents' illness or watching your financial dreams fall apart.

We all know pain, and I will never think that my pain is any better or worse than yours. Candidly, it's not our job to compare our pain to others'. The second we play the comparison game and try to one-up each other, no one wins.

However, it is our role to own our values and choose what we want to do in our lives. In 1980, a group of teenagers gave us hope by giving the entire country something to rally around. They reminded us that even today, David could beat his Goliath.

Well, the puck is about to drop, and the game is about to begin. Today is a new day, and yesterday is in the past. So, are you ready to play the game? Do you have the right perspective? How about the right attitude? Have you prepared for the game of life? Are you taking care of yourself so that you can be your very best?

Finally, who or what in your life is your Russian hockey team? What can you do today to start a new tradition? Just like that packed Lake Placid arena, who do you need to cheer you on and accompany you on your journey? It's your life, your game and your choice.

DAY 23: RETIREMENT

I retired this year, but I'm not talking about my career. You see, I love what I do too much to ever consider retirement, and I've playfully told my company that they will have to kick me out before I retire.

So, while it wasn't as extreme a transition as retiring from my job, I was still emotional because I retired from something that I had been involved in for 21 years. 21 years as a high school tennis coach meant a lot of sun; a lot of mentoring; sore arms from hitting tennis balls and countless life-changing, values-defining memories.

I loved coaching tennis. I suppose it was the chess-like thrill of putting the right players in the right positions, and the relational dynamics of aligning the right doubles teams. I also loved adjusting players' strategies on the fly in the midst of a match. Finally, coaching deeply aligned with my study of positive sports psychology. I could focus on the strengths of my players, and in a short period of time, bring together a group and get them aligned with a vision in a sport that is mostly individual.

I should mention that I didn't retire because I was sick of coaching or tired of the sport. Rather, it was simply time for me to look at new ways to grow and realign my life with the values I profess.

That said, it's been fun to look back on two decades of coaching a sport and thinking about the hundreds of boys and girls I learned from (and with). When I first started coaching, I wasn't much older than many of my players, while in my final year of coaching, a number of players were younger than my kids!

I've also reflected on how different I am today from when I started. Over the years, I have had to learn to coach differently and adjust my perspective. To be honest, a lot of these changes came from my growing more comfortable in my skin and allowing others' voices to be heard. I learned to channel my players' leadership skills and use their voices for the good of the team. Finally, I playfully accepted that I was slower, had far less hair and wasn't in as good shape, but none of that changed my love of the game. None of that changed my love of coaching.

I can also admit that for years, coaching was more about me than the kids. Coaching allowed me to stay connected to a sport that I would have had a hard time leaving, and in fact, this had a lot to do with where I placed my identity. But over time, I learned that tennis had no effect on my character. Sadly, many other coaches choose not to make that adjustment to their coaching values and perspectives. Their identity is far too wrapped up in the success or failure of the team. It's no surprise that the coaches who live with those values (or lack of values) are the ones who yell, swear and belittle their players the most. I suppose that's the danger of putting your identity into what you do rather than who you are.

Retiring from a sport that meant so much to me is not something I have taken lightly. The sense of community and involvement in activities like tennis give us life and fill us up. They get us out of bed in the morning and increase our daily purpose. If we simply close the door and choose not to fill that void, it will hurt us more than it will help.

As of today, I haven't fully figured out how to replace the values connection that coaching provided. That said, I've spent a lot of time learning to take better care of myself, and I am soaking up yoga and cooking. I've also become a "track dad" and love watching my son Tyler run hurdles. In fact, he runs faster than I'd have ever thought possible for a member of the Matson family! And finally, I'm writing more and striving to use my words to mentor more than just the students and players on my court.

The reality is that closure doesn't have to be bad. In fact, it could be one of the best things you ever do. The challenge is in figuring out when to close the chapter, and in accepting which life perspective to assume as you move forward.

Some of you have been giving to an organization just like I did with my coaching, and it's time to hand off the baton and let someone else carry on your legacy. By giving up your role, you are offering someone else the chance to have their life altered by what changed yours.

Some of you need to reprioritize the values that you profess and remember that not all of our values can win all the time. I retired from girls' tennis years ago, right before Morgan started playing, because I wanted to be her dad more than her coach. Are you willing to do the same and move on from something that you love? It might be your career, your role on a board, weekly tutoring, a book club or an additional certificate. Closure can be very difficult, but if your commitment is pulling you away from what is truly important to your heart and soul, then it may be time to create that closure. It's one thing to profess values, but it's a very different act to align our lives with them.

So, as you reflect today, think about what you need to retire from? And if you do retire, what will you add to your life that will allow you to feel more values-aligned? Finally, who can you mentor and be mentored by so that you continue to share your insight and grow? How can you continue to live in alignment with your life purpose?

DAY 24: PETER PAN

I grew up in a suburb of Minneapolis, in a city known for its athletic and academic traditions. My parents went to the same high school, and my grandfather was an elected member of one of the original school boards there. Every year, the district receives numerous awards for its high retention rates and academic prowess.

It's a school that I am proud to have attended, but the reality is that no school is a perfect fit for everyone. When you are enrolled in a school that caters to high-performing students and you aren't a high-performing student yourself, you stick out like a sore thumb.

When I was in high school, the administration allowed for weighted GPAs. This meant that if you took a more advanced course, "extra credit" would be factored into your GPA. As a result, our graduating class saw more than 50 students (out of 600) graduate with over a 4.0 GPA.

It's safe to say that I was not a part of that group of 50, and in fact, I graduated with a borderline GPA between a C+ and a B-. That academic mark of excellence put me in the bottom 25% of my graduating class. This was a fact that made me insecure at that stage in my life, but today I wear it like a badge of honor.

Simply put, thank goodness our high school GPAs aren't directly associated with our success or failure in life! Somehow I've become a high-functioning adult with graduate degrees, and I live as a subject matter expert on leadership in the world of education. Somehow that C+ didn't define me then, and it doesn't define me today.

Yet, somehow we live in an age where we give scores and rankings far too much credit. I repeat, your high school GPA doesn't show me whether you will be academically successful, and your company's internal ranking system doesn't show me whether you are a successful leader within your organization. Though scores and GPAs do provide a starting point for conversation, and we can never lose sight of that, we need to break free from the habit of stressing over one bad score or one bad grade. Scores and rankings don't define us, so make sure not to define yourself by them.

Looking back, the challenge of being academically average in a high school full of future Ivy Leaguers, doctors and lawyers is that you need to find other ways to be unique and known. Though we should all strive to be known for our authenticity, this is a challenging feat for most high school students.

I played college tennis, but the reality was that there were quite a few stars on my high school team. So in class, instead of having the spotlight on my athletic or academic achievements for all my peers to see, I took great pride in being a class clown. As a result, I spent many hours in detention throughout my school years. There I was, sitting with kids who had been in fights or gotten caught cheating, and I was there because I couldn't bite my tongue in class. In high school, you cannot letter in being witty, and though I made some of my teachers smile, being a smart aleck didn't add much to the learning environment.

The reality was — and is — that I love to laugh and make others laugh. My friends and I would try to outdo each other and see who could embarrass one another the most.

Whether skating around the lakes in a rainbow wig and a Speedo, or wearing outdated disco clothes, we loved to make others laugh.

One of our favorite things to do was to film others' reactions to us, and we even created a "greatest hits" tape of these moments. The local mall was one of our favorite filming spots. One of us would step into an elevator with a hidden video camera, and we would wait until the elevator was full before we started filming. Then, right before the doors shut, I would get on last. I would stand there with the biggest smile you've ever seen, facing everyone as the doors shut behind me. People didn't know what to do! I was breaking the rules. You don't stand there facing people in an elevator. No, you turn around and look up like everyone else.

What they didn't realize was that when I got in the elevator on the first floor, I had reached over and hit the buttons for the second and third floors. It must have seemed like an eternity for the other people in the elevator, most of whom didn't know how to react to this tall man grinning at them, but the experience was just a few seconds of awkwardness. In fact, I loved watching their relief as I got off the elevator, taking a swift step backward on the second floor. What they didn't know was that I would dart to the stairs, and when the doors opened again on the third floor, there I'd be! Standing there right in front of the other passengers in the elevator, I would playfully say, "You were talking about me, weren't ya?" The majority of these people would burst into laughter, and the rest would rush off as quickly as possible, avoiding eye contact with me at all costs. But these moments of laughter drove me, and they still do today.

So here it is… I'm just going to say it. I wish that I were best friends with Peter Pan, and I wish that I were a member of the Lost Boys. I still want to laugh and play jokes on other people, just like the Lost Boys modeled for us. That class clown side of me still exists, and yet — when did we stop laughing and get so serious?

Think about it. When was the last time you had a hard laugh? The kind of laugh that makes your stomach ache, and you want to make it stop in fear of pulling a muscle. When was the last time you went out of your way to make others laugh? If laughter is the best medicine, then we need to incorporate more healing into our culture.

Can we just stop taking life so seriously and learn how to laugh again? We need to learn from Peter Pan and never lose that childlike lens. A lens that allows us to see the world with wonder, without worrying about what others think.

The next time you walk past a swing set, go sit on it. Maybe that's as far as you'll get the first time around, but I encourage you to start pumping those legs a bit and feel the butterflies in your stomach. Sit and watch the kids around you laugh, run and jump. Start stepping in puddles again. In fact, I encourage you to JUMP in them instead!

As you begin your day, ask yourself what you can do to put a smile on your face. What could you do tomorrow to make yourself laugh? Where can you go that will bring out your childlike side? Is there a zoo nearby? A science museum? Finally, think about a movie that reminds you of being a kid — and go see it. Today is a day for laughter. It is a day to smile and embrace our inner Peter Pan.

DAY 25: MY CLEANSE FOR PEACE

There isn't one person in this world who wakes up and thinks, *I hope today is a stressful, chaotic day. A day that brings me anxiety.* Well, maybe there are people like that, but if they exist, I would like to keep my distance from them. Though their views are rarely as extreme as my example, those who seek drama are contagious. But to the rest of us — to those of us who would love to reduce the chaos in our lives — I wonder how what we focus on every day adds or detracts from who we seek to be. The reality is, I need to cleanse, and maybe you do too?

Do you really need all of those clothes? If not, can you donate them and give them to someone who needs them more than you do? Ask yourself when you last wore that shirt, and if you can't remember, get rid of it! When I clean out my closet, I think about the person who will wear what I'm getting rid of. I picture the excitement they will feel when they put on that pair of pants for the first time. You can create so much joy, and by getting rid of that closet clutter, you will calm your spirit by making fewer decisions in the morning. Less is more when it comes to tranquility.

Do you really need all that stuff in storage? Last year, I opened box after box and found receipts from over 20 years ago, old bed frames with missing parts and enough Easter baskets to sponsor a neighborhood egg hunt. Simply put, I found that I had too much stuff, and every time I walked into that space, I thought to myself, *I need to clean up this area.* (It had been 15 years since I'd gone through it last!) We ended up throwing out, donating and giving some of our stuff away to friends, and when I walk into that space now, I feel much more calm. Not only that, but I managed to get rid of memories that were better left in the past. Items linked to a different Tom — a Tom I had moved on from. I like who I am today, and seeing some of those old pictures and books caused me to spiral. GET RID OF THEM! Close that chapter. Like and love who you are today, and keep looking for ways to grow as you move forward.

What about all of those piles on your desk? Do you really need all that stuff? When you walk into work and see all that clutter, do you attempt to push everything farther to the side? What would happen if your company asked you to change offices? Would you keep all of that stuff you have? Gosh, look at all these pens from conferences you have attended. Is that a spork and five spoons in that drawer? Looks like you have a lot of squishy balls to help you relax, but they are hidden at the back of your bottom drawer. I wonder if they are truly helping your stress? Throw, throw and throw. Give away books you haven't touched in years and let others learn from the writers who have challenged you. Shift your space from files and piles to a room of creativity. Add a whiteboard, get multicolored pens, put up a picture of a place you love and make your office a positive space where you can find the good and piggyback off ideas that will allow your mind to wander in new directions.

Would you be willing to shift to a stand-up desk or a bike desk? If you are going to stand, then get a balance board as well to make it fully healthy. Right now I'm writing from a walking treadmill desk, and I take about 10,000 steps every two hours. I've found that when I'm walking and talking, my energy flows much better. I feel better about my body, my health and my overall productivity. I saved up for it, and this desk has been life-changing for me — especially on those beautiful winter days in Minnesota when it's just too cold to get outside. Around the space, I have pictures from the

North Shore of Lake Superior and scents that remind me of pine trees and the outdoors. I do my best writing in here, and there isn't a pile to be found around me.

What about your email? Do you really need over 100 emails saved in your inbox? I used to think so. I thought that I would need to come back to old emails over and over again as I went about my work. This seems to have been a reoccurring thought in my mind: *Someday I'll need this.* But then, I started to delete emails, and no one ever came back to ask for them. So, I deleted more of them, and now I never have more than 10 or so emails in my inbox. That's it! When I have more, it's just chaos that I don't need. There were no battle plans for a secret death star in there. There wasn't anything as groundbreaking as a new kind of brain surgery. Honestly, I'm not THAT important, and I don't need to be creating a false sense of value by saving emails. My value isn't in what I save, but in who I am and how I align my life.

The next time you place something in a file, think about whether you really need it. Can you recycle it instead? The next time you put something you've deemed important away, remind yourself that you probably won't need it again. Less is more when it comes to creativity, a mindful life and a cleansed soul. What could you throw away today? What single area could you cleanse? What chapter of your life do you need to close? What can you throw away that reminds you of that season? We are blessed the way we are. No matter what apartment, house, room or space we have, our shelter is a blessing. Look around today and tell yourself what you are thankful for in the space around you. Celebrate, cleanse and refocus your mind and soul.

DAY 26: LITERALLY

Can we talk about the word "literally"? How in the world have we created a word that so many of us misuse? Can we talk about the difference between the words literally and figuratively? When you say to me, "I'm literally drooling at the mouth when I think about that meal last night," and then I look at your dry mouth, I'm disappointed. I'm not sure you meant to say that you were literally drooling; rather, I think that you were speaking in the metaphorical sense. And I sincerely hope you're joking when you say, "I'm literally dying!" For some reason, the word literally has *literally* become overused.

At a recent conference I attended, the speaker was trying to make a bold point about the data when he announced to all of us, "All I want to say is... you're screwed... literally!" He presented a great argument that revealed we are in trouble, and that the path we are on is a dead end. The speaker had us hook, line and sinker, but he ruined his speech with that last word: *literally*. We all glanced sheepishly at one another, yet none of us wanted to make eye contact with the stranger sitting next to us. (Talk about awkward!) I just wish we knew how to use that word correctly, because it can be perfect in the right context! That said, the next time you talk about the growth of your company, avoid telling us that you were "literally exploding." That's just sick and wrong!

Have you laughed today? Have you let out a good, hard belly laugh? Well, it's time to do so! Break out your favorite funny movie. Read a story that makes you laugh. Life is short, so loosen up, smile and laugh!

DAY 27: ART AND SHIRLEY

I met Art and Shirley when I was in my 20s and had just pur-chased my first house. It was a 1950s single-owner home on half an acre of land, filled with apple trees, flowing rhu-barb, raspberry bushes and two giant pine trees. The vision of apple pie, rhubarb streusel and raspberry jam danced through my mind as we sat signing paper after paper at our closing.

The home was blocks away from a hiking trail that mean-dered through the woods, and two parks with walking paths and play equipment. Central Park, the farther of the two, had an old-fashioned rocket ship with built-in ladders and metal decks to soak up the view. It brought me back to my child-hood so much that I decided to try climbing the structure with the kids one day. Given my height, I was convinced that they were going to have to either cut me out or lube me up with butter to slide me out of those metal decks. It clearly wasn't my best dad moment, but gosh, I loved that park.

I also loved our neighbors, and I especially loved Art and Shirley. Their house was directly across from ours, and they had lived in the neighborhood for their entire lives. When we met them, they had just celebrated Art's 80th birthday. In fact, they had saved up for a flagpole so that Art could fly his American flag with pride. They were incredible role models for us as we raised our kiddos, and they always made us feel like we were a part of their family. They brought us cookies, fresh lemonade and plants from their garden. They modeled what true community is supposed to feel like. We borrowed sugar, got each other's mail when we traveled and made sure we were always there when we needed each other.

Our 50-year age difference didn't stop a thriving friendship from forming.

Of course, it didn't feel like Art was 80. In the summer, his yard was always perfect, while I spent my Saturdays mowing a frustratingly impossible lawn. Plus, those apple trees I'd been dreaming of produced the scariest bees I've ever seen, and boy did they get angry when I got too close. Meanwhile, Art's apple trees, yard and landscaping were straight out of a magazine.

I still remember our first big snowfall that year. I woke up "early" on a Saturday (at 9 a.m.) and decided to shovel Art and Shirley's driveway before my own. I bundled up so tight that with my scarf and jacket on, I could hardly move my arms. I went out to my garage, got my shovel and walked across the street to find the most perfectly shoveled driveway I'd ever seen. It looked like Art had picked up every snowflake with a pair of tweezers. But then, I looked to my right and saw Art shoveling the neighbor's driveway as well. I felt a tear freeze against my face, for I knew I was in the midst of shoveling perfection. When Shirley looked outside and saw me standing in her driveway, she waved me in for a cup of hot cocoa.

After 20 minutes of struggling to remove my jacket, scarf, hat, boots and choppers, I sat down at their counter. When you are sitting with someone older than you, it's important to always take the time to ask questions and truly listen. So, I asked Shirley how the neighborhood had changed over the years, and her answer surprised me. "Oh Tom," she said with a smile that lit up the room, "our neighborhood used to be like a family, and within one year that all changed." I waited on the edge of my seat to hear what had changed Parker Avenue. "It was the year that we all got central air conditioning." When Shirley paused and silence filled the air, I honestly didn't know how to respond. Air conditioning? That was it? That was the big change?

"How did air conditioning change the neighborhood, Shirley?" I asked. She explained that the minute the homes were cool, everyone went inside. They stopped sitting on their front porches and drinking lemonade together, and the kids started to play inside far more than they played outside. Before Shirley knew it, the neighbors had stopped gathering outside and truly getting to know one another.

"I miss sitting with my neighbors, Tom," she said. "I hope you will forever go outside and not hide out in your home. I want to get to know you, and I want you to get to know the gift of being outside."

After I wiped the whipped cream from my top lip and gave Shirley a hug, I walked out the door a changed man.

In our 10-minute conversation, Shirley reminded me to get off my Atari and Nintendo and go outside. She reminded me how important it is to soak up this beautiful world. She taught me what it means to be a neighbor who is present and truly gets to know the people around me.

So, every day I get outside, and I walk and hike. If it's cold, I bundle up, and if it's too hot, I don't walk very far. When I get outside, I love the sensation of the breeze whipping through my hair, and I love the feel of the colorful leaves crunching underneath my feet in the fall. And in the spring, I love my watery eyes and runny nose as my allergies react to the new beauty appearing around me. Not even those allergies can stop me from living out what Shirley taught me. Her words were just too powerful.

Shirley taught me how to enjoy the outdoors, while Art taught me how to serve my neighbors. Both Shirley and Art showed me how a neighborhood can feel like a family. So, what can you learn about these things? When was the last time you went for a walk and left your phone at home so you could truly enjoy the outdoors? When was the last time you brought flowers or cookies over to your neighbor? How can you serve and show affection to the people around you today? We often seek to volunteer and serve, yet we forget to bestow that same love, respect, kindness and impact upon our neighbors.

DAY 28: RUDY MOMENTS

Right now I'm flying from Minneapolis to Colorado, and I decided to use my flight time to rest and disconnect from work. Sometimes flying gives me my very best writing, and other times, it is a fantastic place for mental quiet. Due to my busy schedule, today was a movie day, and I put on my headphones right away to let the person beside me know that I wasn't available to talk. The headphones weren't attached to anything, but I needed to hide.

We all need to hide at times. To take deep breaths. Sometimes we need to lie on the floor and meditate. We need time to let our hearts align with our thoughts. And yet, the busier we become as a culture, the more these times get pushed aside, and we begin to rely on bathroom breaks as our only quiet time. While the bathroom is an awkward place to hide, sometimes it's the only space where we can truly be alone.

The reality is that we all need alone time. In fact, it's a healthy value to create in our life and model for others. However, let's not get confused between the words alone and lonely. Though they sound similar, they have very different meanings. Being alone means we are truly alone, and that we are not around other people, while thousands can surround us and yet we still feel lonely. Creating healthy alone time is an essential value when it comes to refocusing and realigning our lives.

When I fly, I'm surrounded by others, but even in this space I can close off the world around me and journal, listen to music, rest, close my eyes and dream, or in this case, escape to a new world. Sometimes flying leaves me feeling recharged, while other times it can feel lonely (even though I'm surrounded by other people — in a very small space, I might add).

Today I was watching one of my favorite movies of all time. *Rudy* is about the life of Rudy Ruettiger, who dreamed of playing football at Notre Dame despite a lack of family support, limited financial resources and academic challenges due to a learning disability. With the help and sponsorship of a local priest, Rudy enrolled in community college to earn the grades to get into his dream school. Then, after years of rejection, he finally received an acceptance letter from Notre Dame. And that's where the tears began. Not his tears, mind you, but mine. I couldn't stop the tears from flowing, and they continued to gain strength as I watched Rudy rush home to share the news with his family. He went right to his father's steel mill, and when Mr. Ruettiger announced his son's accomplishment over the loudspeaker, that was it. My streaming tears transformed into full-on sobbing. I lost all control, and no matter how hard I tried, I couldn't stop myself. I'm talking gasping noises, a runny nose and no ability to communicate.

Why was I so emotional? I've seen this movie roughly 100 times, and I had never before felt so overwhelmed by the emotional side of it. Well, I came to find out that these intense emotions weren't just feelings I experienced on flights. In 2011, the airline Virgin Atlantic surveyed customers to describe their on-flight emotional experiences. Overall, 55% of travelers said they had "experienced heightened emotions while flying," and a striking 41% of men stated that they had "buried themselves in blankets to hide tears in their eyes from other passengers." Women, on the other hand, were more likely to pretend they had something in their eye. Regardless, it turned out that I was far from alone.

I think that more than just the altitude and touching movies can trigger an emotional response while flying. Elaine Iljon Foreman, a cognitive behavioral therapist who runs Freedom To Fly courses for frightened air passengers, links midair emotional responses to the feelings of being away from the safety of familiar places, the isolation of being away from the people you love and the mental struggle of traveling in unstructured time. You pile all of those emotional responses together, and travelers have a heightened emotional response at over 39,000 feet.

But maybe there is more than lack of control and fear overwhelming travelers? Maybe those emotions build until they reach a spot where they need to be released? As I buckle my 6'4" frame into my seat — a seat that appears to have been built for someone far smaller than I am — maybe all the emotions that I've been pushing aside spill over because that is what my body needs.

Every single day, as we live the lives we are meant to live, we are like sponges taking in all that we see and feel. The car that cut you off earlier, you sure felt that. That stressful work meeting, well, those emotions are still there. That comment a worker made to a stranger in front of you in line — that sure didn't feel fair. Cleaning up after others, coworkers who seem to need you rather than care about you — those emotions pile up until they simply need to escape.

I suppose I didn't need a Rudy moment on the airplane to feel all that I was feeling, but I haven't been very kind to myself lately. Less journaling, fewer walks, quicker (and less healthy) meals on the go and a focus that is about appeasing others rather than practicing self-care. My shoulders have been feeling tight as I pull the weight of others' expectations.

Actually, I think I did need Rudy today. Those emotions needed to flow, and so do yours. Emotions are freeing. In fact, your emotions are a gift, and they should not be buried away where nobody can see or hear them. You deserve to be heard.

You deserve to share all that you are feeling, and to welcome others to share their feelings with you. Who could you reach out to today to share what's in your heart? How can you communicate that need so it's clear what you are asking for? Who could you call today and ask how their heart is and what they have been feeling lately? We all need Rudy moments, and you can create them for yourself and others. But for now, it's time for me to finish the movie and cheer for Rudy as he continues to achieve his goals.

DAY 29: PERSPECTIVES IN THE WOODS

I just returned home from the Boundary Waters in Northern Minnesota. The Boundary Waters are thousands of acres of woods, plus thousands of lakes near the border of Minnesota and Canada. Most of the lakes are only accessible by canoe or kayak, and the silence and peace of the Boundary Waters Canoe Area (BWCA) is a gift. You can go days without seeing another soul, and the wildlife is in abundance. On the first day of our trip, my soon-to-be adult son was still sleeping while I sat in a chair and gazed through the picture window upon Loon Lake. We had arrived later in the day, and I hadn't been able to appreciate the lake like I had hoped. Though I awoke to a blanket of fog covering the water that morning, the sun had begun to break through the clouds and filter into our cabin, and I couldn't wait to see the lake again. There is just something about a lake that goes on for miles and miles.

I sipped my coffee and took it all in, watching the squirrels run across our deck. Earlier, I had seen a deer bound across the land. I even heard the call of a loon from my bed that morning, and to this day, I consider it one of the most tranquil sounds in all of nature.

Like a typical resort, the guests are asked to write about what they loved and did on their Boundary Waters adventure. You see, while the majority of people canoe in with their tent and food on their back, I'm past that stage in life, and I love the joy of a hot meal at the lodge and a roof over my head at night.

The guestbook is a glimpse back in time... 10 years of stories and perspectives. Some are emotional. Others are funny. Others more are about renewing love. Several touch on the healing process after loss. I read about one woman who, upon receiving a breast cancer diagnosis, retreated to the Boundary Waters before beginning her treatment. Her words exuded fear of the future, and yet they were dripping with courage, hope and an adventuresome spirit as she prepared for her battle.

A younger child wrote another entry about what it was like to see the woods and lakes for the first time. Growing up, the girl's mother had stayed at the lodge (it dated back to the early 1900s), but since the young girl lived in Chicago, this was a brand new world for her. She loved the stand-up paddleboards the most, as well as the daily walks she took with her parents. Both her mother and father would grab her hands at the same time, and with a giant swing of their arms, she would soar into the air. Their carefree family dynamic added so much depth to her story.

There were many other stories, of course. Some visited the Boundary Waters to escape the chaos of their world back home. Some wanted a quiet place to heal after the end of a relationship. Some made the drive to carry on traditions, and others shared that they simply needed a private place to cry.

Yet, everyone writes in the same guestbook. The same location. The same view. Different perspectives. Different needs. I wonder how many others have sat in this space and talked about life with a loved one?

That was my hope for this week. To not only experience the beauty of the Boundary Waters with Tyler, but to get to know him on a deeper level and understand his character, values and life perspectives. I imagined the two of us sitting in a boat and talking for hours on end. I imagined how close I would feel with him and what it would mean for our relationship. These were all healthy hopes and perspectives, but they were *my* hopes and perspectives. They were not necessarily Tyler's.

It would have been easy to shut down after our first meal together. When we took a seat on the couches in the lodge, the conversation didn't flow like I had hoped. It would have been easy to get mad at him and push him to talk. We often do that, don't we? We overreact when we don't get what we want, and since we read about the need for depth in so many books, we force it. In fact, I still remember sitting in a cabin in Wisconsin and going through a marriage book. The awkwardness of the questions was jarring, as was the forced attempted intimacy and what felt like a desire to flip the switch, break open the book and feel close. But that's not how life is. Life is messier than that, and when we sit down with another person, they bring their perspective and lens to the table as well.

Sitting across from my 17-year-old, one would assume that I'd have known his needs. The fact that he wanted to come and spend this time with me communicated volumes. The fact that he was excited to be with his dad in the woods rather than with his friends was a testament to his love and how he felt about our relationship. Yet sadly, I missed his nonverbal cues and remained fixated on my need for life-changing, tear-jerking talks. These were my needs... not his needs. So, what did a teen boy want? Tyler wanted to hike, swim, play cards, canoe, explore and soak up the world around him. His needs were focused on gaining new life perspectives and stories to share with his friends, and possibly his own kids someday. The fish we caught would get bigger with every story, and the hikes we took would grow longer.

We all bring our own perspective to life and to our relationships. But sometimes, like at the beginning of this trip, our selfishness clouds our lens and we fail to see what's right in front of us. Our needs are like the fog that keeps us from seeing the beauty and peace of the lake. We need to learn how to change our perspective and view life from a different angle. People have different hopes and needs — including

91

those who have sat in this very chair — and that's perfectly okay. In many ways, it's what makes life interesting. It's what makes life a true gift.

That morning at breakfast, instead of trying to force Ty to talk, I found our deck of cards and we started a gin rummy tournament. Two out of three games at meals, and then more board games and puzzles at night in our cabin. And a funny thing happened when I chose to shift my perspective and let go of my needs that were getting in the way of our trip. You see, Tyler and I began to talk. It wasn't that Ty hadn't wanted to talk before, but that my son prefers to talk when he is busy. Of course — I knew that! But I had forgotten, and I almost missed the chance to learn more about the amazing parts of who he is. So all week long, the words flowed while we hiked. When we caught this 14-inch (and still growing) Northern Pike, our laughter filled the air and the shared experience filled our souls. The irony of our love for adventure was that neither one of us cared to touch the fish! Maybe we weren't stereotypical adventurers, but we didn't care. No, what we cared about was being together. And what really changed our trip was when I chose to change my perspective and meet Tyler halfway. I've missed some great moments in the past because I refused to make compromises, and as a result, my insecurity, fears and selfishness kept me from soaking up the gifts in front of me. But not on this trip. In fact, as I look back at my pictures, I smile and remember how this trip changed our relationship. The fog lifted and life went on, and so will yours.

Today, how can you change your perspective on a relationship and find a way to meet the other person halfway? How can you see the good in those in front of you and identify their needs by asking the right questions? Finally, what fog is clouding your life today that you need swept away so that you can see the beauty in front of you once more? The choice is yours.

DAY 30: WRITE YOUR LEGACY

I don't write because I think I'm the best writer in the world. I don't write because I think it's going to make me rich. I don't write because I think my words are more profound than the words of other authors. I don't write because I think my words are more important than yours. I don't write because I have an ego, and I certainly don't feel the need to brag that I'm a published author.

I write because I love to write. Writing makes me happy. It's therapeutic, and it's good for my mind. I write because it allows me to reflect on my life and hold up a mirror that I can look into and share what I see and learn. I write because I can, and because I love words so much. Writing is my chance to playfully weave my thoughts into ideas — ideas that I sincerely hope will make you think and reflect. But more than any other reason, I write because it's my way of leaving my legacy.

So what about you? What do you want to do to leave your mark on the world? In order for you to determine what kind of legacy you want to leave, first you need to clarify what values you want to live. A life with no defined values will be a confusing one, and it will be difficult for your loved ones to know whether you fulfilled your dreams and goals.

Values cannot simply be proclaimed, for they need to be sorted based on what matters most to you. For example, as a former tennis coach, I loved every bit of that journey, and it mattered a great deal to me. BUT, it didn't matter more than my family, friends, views on well-being, values aligned with positive psychology and my love and protection of nature.

All of those values matter FAR more than coaching tennis ever did, and yet if I passed away tomorrow and all everyone talked about was my tennis coaching, I would think that I had missed my mark on the world. Somehow, I must have communicated that my tennis coaching trumped those other values, and that would be wrong.

As you consider your legacy, think of a sentence or two that defines your life purpose. Put into words for others what you want to be known for. What do you want to be remembered for? What matters most?

Then, could you take the values you proclaim and put them in order? This is where the majority of us fail. We proclaim a list of so many values that they can't all win, and then we appear inconsistent to others. Plus, it is hard to understand why parts of our lives feel misaligned if we choose not to prioritize our values.

Two of my friends are dating after their previous marriages ended in divorce. One of them has two children from his previous marriage, while the other never had children with her former spouse. They have been dating for a few years now, and they authentically love being together. If they had roughly 10 values, I would guess that 70% of them are in alignment. Health and exercise matter to both of them, as do travel and shared experiences, and education as well. The list goes on and on. Yet, they are struggling and still trying to figure out if they can make it as a couple. You see, she would love to have kids with her new partner, but he is older and already has two children, and he isn't sure that he wants to have more. They are stuck. The vast majority of their values are aligned, but a child is one of her top core values, while a child is much lower on his list. Again, it's not that their values aren't aligned. Rather, when they sorted their values, the order of those values mattered, and this discrepancy became the foundation of their pain as a couple.

A values sort also reveals itself in the connection between our jobs and our work culture. We look at the mission of the company we work for, and we read those words and fully see ourselves in that mission. Then we arrive at work and find a disconnect, and over time we find ourselves confused by how we feel at the office. Our stress levels rise over time, and we start getting sick more and more often. And yet, we keep coming back to that mission statement! It looks like we could have written it ourselves, so why do we feel such a bold disconnect? The reason for our pain is exposed in the way we rank our values. For you, the mission wins, and for the company, revenue wins; and while you spend your time focusing on projects that align with your mission, the company is looking for revenue from you. The vast majority of your organizational values might have been aligned, but those top core values were off, and now you are left with a choice. You can change the order of your values and risk sacrificing your authenticity, or you can seek those values elsewhere.

Legacy is about knowing yourself and creating a sorted values list to serve as the guiding principles for your life. When our values are sorted, we are more open to feedback because we can no longer hide from our true selves. Sorted values help us determine whether a company or relationship is right for us. In addition, written and shared values allow us to help others go through life with us.

Can you take some time away and brainstorm your core values? Can you put those values into order? Again, not all of your values can win, and by prioritizing them, you can better sort your decisions and align them with what you hold dear in your life. Finally, can you think of your life mission statement that aligns with how you imagine your legacy? Simply put, what is the ultimate impact of your life? How do you want people to remember you?

ACKNOWLEDGEMENTS

To my family, who has continued to be there for me each and every step of the way — thank you for our Sunday dinners, our walks and the time we've spent processing life, patterns and values together. So much of what I have written here comes from you. I truly love learning with and from you! You have all remained encouraging and constantly remind me what is important in life.

To my friends from all areas of my life, and from all over the country — for some of you, we have gone through life together for just a few years, while I have spent a lifetime with others. No matter how long we've known each other, there is something in all of you that keeps us close, and it comes down to aligned values and a growth-based lens on life. You all make me better, and I couldn't imagine my life without you.

To my Gallup friends, with whom I spend the majority of my daily life — you have taught me to soar with my strengths. Thanks to you, I have learned how to look in the mirror, own my actions and live a thriving life. I'm honored to work with each of you, and to count you as dear friends. What a gift of community that you provide!

Finally, to Maddie Cohen, my editor. When we first met, I told you that I was looking for a true writing partner, and you've played that role and provided far more than I could have ever imagined. I'm so thankful for you and for sharing with me your writing and editing gifts. I've been honored to see your incredible talents in action. Thank you for your mentoring, partnership and friendship!

AUTHOR'S BIO

Tom Matson is a speaker, executive coach, author and leadership expert. A seasoned TEDx speaker, Tom presents to thousands of people each year about leadership, well-being and behavioral economics. He challenges his listeners to become authentic leaders who are committed to developing their strengths and creating a thriving life.

Tom coached high school tennis for more than 20 years and was named the Minnesota Assistant Tennis Coach of the Year in 2011. He has sat on the Board of Directors of the United States Tennis Association's Northern Tennis Foundation, the National Advisory Board of Tennis and Life Camps and has taken on numerous leadership roles for the Sigma Chi Fraternity. He is the author of *Unfrozen: A Father's Reflections on a Brain Tumor Journey*.

Tom earned a bachelor's degree in communications, a master's degree in organizational leadership and a graduate certificate in positive psychology. He and his family live in the Twin Cities, in the beautiful Land of 10,000 Lakes.

CPSIA information can be obtained
at www.ICGtesting.com
Printed in the USA
BVOW08*0949171216
471116BV00004B/34/P

9 781635 054491